Dr. Marci Tilghman Bryant

101

Ways To Keep Going
When The Going Gets Tough

101 Ways to Keep Going, When the Going Gets Tough!
By Dr. Marci Tilghman-Bryant
Cover Created & Designed by Leroy Grayson
Logos by Andre M. Saunders/Jess Zimmerman
Editor: Anelda L. Attaway

© 2020 Dr. Marci Tilghman-Bryant
ISBN 978-1-954425-03-3
Library of Congress Control Number: 2020925504

All rights reserved. This book is protected by the copyright laws of the United States of America. This book may not be copied or reprinted for commercial gain or profit. The use of short quotations or occasional page copying for personal or group study is permitted and encouraged. Permission will be granted upon request. This book is for Worldwide Distribution and printed in the United States of America, published by Jazzy Kitty Publications utilizing Microsoft Publishing Software.

ACKNOWLEDGMENTS & DEDICATIONS

To all my family and friends who hung in there with me on my late night and early morning talking visuals. This has been a work special to my heart because I have lived it and helped others do the same. I hope that it makes a difference in your life as you keep moving forward toward your destiny.

While all persons who inspired me to write this book are too long to list, there are a few honorable mentions because of your prayers and your gifts of love that has helped this publication become a reality:

- BVT Church Family
- CGM Church Family
- One Bright Hope Theatrical Family
- WOAL Ministries Worship Center

DEDICATION

I dedicate this book to God and everyone that I love.

TABLE OF CONTENTS

INTRODUCTION..i

Poem-Time to Live..ii

CHAPTER 1

Facing Reality; Then on to Boot Camp...............01

CHAPTER 2

Become Even More Determined; Boot Camp.....30

CHAPTER 3

You are Special, Boot Camp................................55

CHAPTER 4

Common Ground, Boot Camp.............................72

Poem-Who is Jesus..89

Contact Information...91

Poem-God Sent His Son My Way........................92

ABOUT THE AUTHOR...................................96

Photo References:...98

INTRODUCTION

Boot camp is where the novice civilian goes to train for the battles ahead. Believers and even those who are not sure what they believe to the fullest need training for living life. Among other things, boot camp teaches discipline. Every soldier needs it to run the course and fight the battle. We are referred to as soldiers in 2 Timothy 2:3, admonishing us to "endure hardship as a good soldier of Jesus Christ."

It is my prayer that this book will help you endure and give you the hope you need to keep going. Giving up on life is not an option for the one who wants the prize.

101 Ways to Keep Going, When the Going Gets Tough is spiritual boot camp. Its design is to toughen you up so that the battles of life will not defeat you.

TIME TO LIVE

In just One Moment
From the Stillness in the Night
The Sound of Morning reaches my Ear
I Look through my Window
A Burst of Light just happens to Appear

And I called my Thoughts
From Yesterday and Wonder Why
I STILL Feel Pain in my Head
Why the Sorrow in my Heart
Oh God, Not Today,
Not Another Day of Dread

And into my thoughts come these words…
There is a Reason for Life

Open wide your Heart, Let Go, and Forgive
Yes, this is the Time Now
The Time for me, you and me to Live!

Life is sometimes so Cruel
With the Curves Tossed in our way
But you've got to Keep On Moving
You can and you must make it through this,
Another day

For this is the Time, your Time
There is a Reason for Life
Open wide your Heart, Let Go, and Forgive
Yes, this is the Time now, the Time to Live!

Now Dash to the Mirror
Take a Good Look at your Face
There is a Reason you are Here
No one but you could have this Certain Space

For before the Beginning of Time
The Infinite one made it so

You've got a Choice, either Wallow in Self Pity
Or live and just let Misery Go

For this is the Time, your Time to Live
There is a Reason for Life
Open wide your Heart, Let Go, and Forgive
Yes, this is the Time Now
The Time for me, you, and me to Live!

You Were Born by the Will of God
To Accomplish MANY things
There is Greatness inside of you…

It will Live on after you
Daily it Shows in Everything that you Do
But you've got to…
Define it, Refine it, Mine it,
And Prime it! It's all inside of you
What's in your way?
Let it Go this Day

Walk On, Stand Tall, Laugh Out Loud
Show forth that Smile in your Heart
Today, you are STILL here,
Today is your Brand-New Start

For this is the Time, your Time,
There is a Reason for your Life
Open wide your Heart Let Go and Forgive
Yes, this is the Time Now
The Time, the Time, your Time, my Time,
Our Time, We've Got to Live!

Let it Go,
Whatever it is that's Holding you Back
Whatever has held you back,
Let it Go
Leave it in your Past

Let Goodness Flow from within
Until it Overflows

And Comes out into your Present
Now is the Time,
To give your Dreams a Chance
Give your Heart a Lift

OPEN WIDE YOUR MOUTH

Say, I Forgive Others
I Forgive Myself
I Forgive and Today,
Yes, Today

I will NOT Walk in Fear, Shame, or Doubt
I WILL LIVE!

I will Trust the Savior of my Soul
For it's my Time
It's my Time to LIVE!!!

CHAPTER 1

Facing Reality; Then on to Boot Camp

If you lived past the age of 13, you know what it's like to want to give up. You have experienced those moments when you just want to disappear…moments when you just want to stop trying altogether.

It's in these times that we often find outside reinforcement less than enough. It either isn't there, or it's as everyone around us is oblivious to our particular needs. "Way to go; good job, keep your chin up, it's okay, don't cry, it's not so bad, look on the bright side, it could have been worst…" and the list of those pat responses go on and on. So, what are we to do, especially when those comments don't work? When we still feel like giving up? We turn to our inner self!

We try hard to cut ourselves off from the pain and disappointments. We try to reason within ourselves, why are these situations happening to us? We try hard to find something to hold on to. But what happens if nothing is there to sustain us? If we can't seem to reach that "center" inside of us that is to steady us, ground us, teach us, help us?

Much in this world seeks to improve us on the outside. But the improvement and strength we need must come from within. If the world hasn't put there the strength and fortitude (and indeed it cannot) that we need to keep going, where then must we find our answer? Where do we go?

We need to deal with revealed truths in order to find what we need! There is truth, and then there is truth that comes from within that enters into our conscious thoughts to enlighten us to the point of rebirth. This new birth is a whole new way of thinking…a way that causes us no longer to just exist but to live.

After all, the truth of our past hasn't been clear enough to help us move away from this present state of disappointment. Thus, this truth alone should make us want to deal a better hand for our future. If we are honest with ourselves, we must admit that we played a major role in getting to where we are right now. And because this book has found your hand and you are taking the time to read it, you are also taking responsibility for changing what you can within your experience, and that my friend is A GOOD THING!

Everything except God has a beginning. Mankind has a beginning, and it goes back to our Creator. He designed us for good. He designed us to live in this *outside* world from *within* ourselves. Somehow in the midst of changing generations, we have forgotten that man is not just the outer shell we see from day to day. He is a fearfully and wonderfully made human being with a complex personality and has, in addition to its body, a soul and spirit.

When life hits hard, it does tend to knock the wind from us. It can also zap our strength and our resolve to go on. Sometimes it causes us to even question our birth…why was I even born?

I have been there before, many times in my life, so it became necessary for me to find that inner calm that was built into my system to help me keep going. And because it works as a byproduct of my faith, I have decided to share it with others. So, take some time, sit down in a quiet place, close your eyes for approximately 30 seconds. Breathe deeply and then turn the first of several pages. Get ready to mount up with wings as like an eagle and SOAR! Today is the day that you begin AGAIN!

1. YOU HAVE A RIGHT TO BE HERE.

You were in the mind of God before you were formed in your mother's womb. Your purpose in the earth is "divine." If you have not found it yet, keep going because your purpose makes living in this world...worthwhile! Everything that has happened to you thus far can work together for your good, no matter how you might feel at this very moment. You are here in the earth at this time because God Himself has willed it to be so! Your task is to believe this to be true!

2. THINK PLEASANT THOUGHTS

Regardless of what you may be feeling right now, allow your mind to go back to a place at a time when you were feeling happy, a time when it felt good just to laugh out loud. Stay there in that place for several minutes. It's good to remember the good times. Remember, as many as you like, this is your time to think on these things…the pure things, the honest things, the good things, those virtuous things that cause you to smile from the inside out.

3. FORGIVE YOURSELF

We make mistakes. It's a fact of life. The world's most renowned people, those whose names we find in our history books, made mistakes. Mistakes help shape us. They teach us what we need to do in order to prepare for a different outcome. Mistakes don't define us; they refine us! Give yourself a hug and say out loud, "It's going to be alright in just a little while!"

"Yes, I've made mistakes, but I am not a mistake!"

4. SAY THIS PRAYER:

God forgive me. Help me forgive myself and anyone else whom I am finding it difficult to forgive. Help me let go of the disappointment and pain. Help me hold on to you. I pray this prayer in the name of Jesus, who is my bridge to you. Amen. Remember, prayer does not have to be fancy or long-winded. Just say what's on your heart when you need to say it.

5. TAKE A WALK THROUGH THE PARK OR AROUND A TRACK.

Don't underestimate the benefits derived from physical movement/exercise. Like your mind and your body needs physical activity. While walking, remember *#2, think pleasant thoughts.* Recite the

Lord's prayer. Make it personal: My Father which art in Heaven, hallowed be thy Name, Thy Kingdom come thy will be done on earth as it is in Heaven. Give me this day, my daily bread, and forgive me my debts as I forgive my debtors. And lead me not into temptation but deliver me from evil for thine is the Kingdom and the power and the glory forever, AMEN.

6. WRITE A LETTER HEARTFELT TO A FRIEND OR RELATIVE WHOM YOU HAVE NOT CONTACTED FOR MORE THAN A YEAR.

Reaching out to someone else will do you a lot of good. As your soul stretches beyond its present set of circumstances, you will find it refreshing to concentrate on something other than your own "woes." Mail the letter!

7. DO SOMETHING FOR SOMEBODY ELSE AND DO IT QUICKLY.

Don't stop to analyze, should I do this or should I do that. Once you see a need, whether it be for a man, woman, boy, or girl, just do it. It could be as simple as helping a child up from a fall to helping a young mother with a housing chore. Cut the grass for a neighbor, take a dog for a walk, buying a cup of coffee for a stranger, just do something for somebody else. You will be amazed at how it will help you get beyond your blues.

8. THANK SOMEONE FOR THEIR KINDNESS THAT THEY HAVE SHOWN YOU.

Be sincere, be specific. Everyone likes to feel appreciated. This can be done in person, by phone, fax, or by email. Do it today. Do it often. If we allow ourselves to look past our moment of disappointment, we will see that others have poured so much into us that we have allowed to go unacknowledged. Let's honor them by telling them how grateful we are for their kindness toward us.

9. REAFFIRM OUT LOUD — "TODAY IS A GOOD DAY, NOT THE BEST OF MY DAYS, BUT A GOOD DAY! I AM ALIVE AND I HAVE ANOTHER CHANCE TO BE FREE!"

You must hear your voice making this declaration. Then once throughout the day. It's like medicine to your soul. After all, this IS the day that the Lord has made and we will rejoice and be glad in it.

10. COOK, BAKE, FIX, OR MIX UP YOUR FAVORITE DISH AND ASK SOMEONE TO SHARE THE MEAL WITH YOU.

No appetite? That's alright; it will help just having someone present with you to enjoy the meal. Any leftovers? Take them to work and share them with your fellow employees. You might be pleasantly surprised to see how many smiles your home-cooked meal will cause to appear. Smiles are contagious. When you see one, give one.

11. PLAY SOME CLASSICAL MUSIC.

So, you don't like classical music! Do it anyway. You need to listen to some music without words, music that will speak to your soul. It will move your thoughts to a better place. Some of the greatest classical music artists are Beethoven, Mozart, Brahms, Bach, Chopin, just to name a few.

12. GO BROWSE AT A BRICK-AND-MORTAR BOOKSTORE.

This is especially effective if you choose a store where you can browse and read and sip on a cup of tea or coffee while you look around. Take your time; spend at least 3 hours in this place. Rushing this experience will not help your mood. Slow down and look, really look at all that is available to you. If, and only if you find something that speaks to your soul, purchase it, but not before you spend some time with it.

13. TAKE A LONG HOT BUBBLE BATH.

This is also a good time to listen to your classical music. Again, don't rush the experience. Try not to think about anything. Let your mind and body just relax in the warm, soothing water.

14. CRY...YES CRY!

Sometimes a good cry is exactly what the patient may need. Just keep crying until you just can't cry anymore. The chances are you will fall asleep afterward and wake up feeling a little more refreshed. Trying to pretend that you don't hurt is not the solution. The pain must be dealt with. You must face it in order to heal.

15. PLAN A TRIP

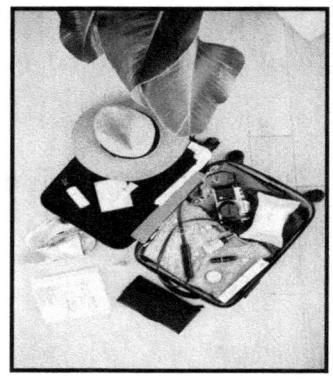

Think about a place that you have always wanted to visit but never been there. Start the research necessary to find out all about this place. Don't worry about when you are going to go or even if you have the finances to get there. This is not the purpose of this exercise. The purpose is to restart your dreams by taking your mind to faraway places. Use the library or the internet to find out as much information as you can about this place you'd like to visit (someday – soon).

16. PICK A MONTH THAT HAS 31 DAYS IN IT AND BEGINNING WITH DAY #1 READ THE BOOK OF PROVERBS (in the Holy Bible) CHAPTER ONE. THEN ON DAY #2 READ THE SECOND BOOK OF PROVERS. ON DAY #3 READ THE THIRD BOOK OF PROVERBS. ETC.

Sunday	Monday	Tuesday	Wednesday	Thursday	Friday	Saturday
27	28	29	30	1	2	3
4	5	6	7	8	9	10
11	12	13	14	15	16	17
18	19	20	21	22	23	24
25	26	27	28	29	30	31

July 2021

Don't shortchange yourself. Do this every single day. Even for those of you who don't like to read, this exercise is excellent therapy. You only have to read one proverb book per day, and when the month is over, you will have to feed your soul a wealth of Godly wisdom that will prove invaluable to your daily living.

17. GO TO A NURSING HOME, AN ASSISTED LIVING FACILITY, OR HOSPITAL AND VOLUNTEER TO READ A BOOK TO SOMEONE BEDRIDDEN

Show up with a book of inspirational poetry and other writings. Spend at least an hour with some you don't know. (Ask the Admin on Duty, who could use a visitor and visit that person or those persons). It's always a good idea to invest into the life and well-being of someone who may be less fortunate than you. We all need help at some point and time. In short, we need each other. Somebody needs you, so go and give yourself away.

18. START YOUR SAVINGS PLAN. FOLLOW THIS SIMPLE STRUCTURED PLAN-YOU WILL BE AMAZED!

Get a legal envelope or a zippered money bag. On day #1, put in $1.00; the next day, double it. On day #2, you now have $2.00. On the next day (day #3), double the $2.00 you have in your envelope (or bag). You now have $4.00. On day #4, double the amount that you have, and you now have $8.00. Continue this process daily until you cannot double your money. On the day that you cannot double what's in the envelope is the day you take 10% of whatever you have accumulated and give it to your church as a tithe, take one dollar away from the amount to begin the process again. With what you have left, treat yourself to something nice.

> **IT'S BETTER TO GIVE THAN RECEIVE ACTS 20:35**

19. GIVE SOMETHING AWAY

It can be anything like clothes, food, shoes, books, money, a blanket, household items, jewelry, etc. just pick something that has value to you and give it away. The gift can be to someone you know, or it can be to a stranger. You decide. However, it must be something that you wouldn't mind receiving for yourself. In short, don't give away anything that you wouldn't want.

20. SAY A PRAYER/THEN SING A SONG

No need to be fancy; just speak what's on your heart and in your mind. It's a good idea to be alone when you do this. Alone time with God, the Father, through His only begotten Son, Jesus, is always good. He loves to hear your voice also, especially when it's singing a praise or worship song. In the book of Psalm, He tells us to make a joyful noise… (Psalm 100) take Him at His word! Sing! Make Noise! God loves hearing your voice.

21. LOOK IN THE MIRROR AND SMILE.

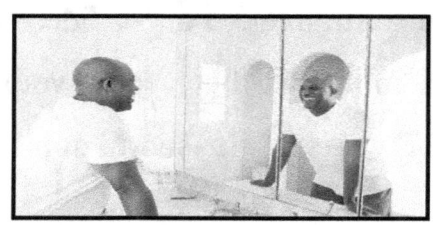

Yes, stand in front of the mirror and take a long look at yourself. You are fearfully and wonderfully made according to the word of God. Smile and hug yourself. And as you stand there, strike a poise. Remind yourself that there is only ONE in this world like you. That's right, just one! You are unique!

22. OPEN THE WINDOWS

It's time to allow the fresh air into your space and into your lungs. Breathe deeply. As the refreshing air comes in, pick up a dust cloth and dust, pick up the broom and sweep. Take out the vacuum and roll it over the carpet. Load the dishwasher; better yet, wash the dishes by hand. Dry them and put them away.

Keep going until all the manual work is done. You will be amazed how much you can accomplish if you just keep going.

23. PICTURE YOUR FUTURE. WHERE DO YOU WANT TO GO FROM HERE?

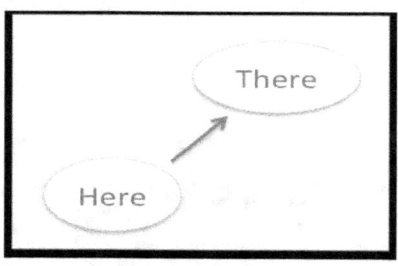

Without a vision, the people (in this case, you) will perish. You will stop growing and stop achieving and reaching for higher heights. Focus on any one or two of those dreams that you have left behind or tucked away. Now is a good time to resurrect that precious vision. What can you now do that you have not done before that will help you take the first step toward that goal? Who do you know who is living your dream? If it was possible for them, it is also possible for you!

24. START A DAILY JOURNAL

Writing down your thoughts can be therapeutic. Keep a small tablet in your pocket or purse. When you find your thoughts flooding your mind, take a few moments to take out a pen and your tablet, and write down your thoughts. Don't worry about editing them at this time. It's important just to get them outside your head. You can re-read what you wrote later, and you will be surprised at how deep you really are. You might discover what really is at the core of your disappointment. Understanding what affects you and how it is affecting you will be of great help to you on this healing journey. After all, you can't fix what you don't realize is in need of repair.

25. FIND A FAITH SCRIPTURE THEN MEDITATE ON IT. READ IT DAILY AND READ IT OFTEN.

You need something of "faith" to hold on to. The world has let you down and you must find a new place to hang your hopes and your dreams. The Bible is full of faith food; it's called the WORD of God. Look through it, you are bound to find something to feed your soul.

26. FIND A MENTOR

Look at those in your immediate circle, then look outside your circle. Find someone whose life and character that you admire. Call them. Invite them to lunch and tell them how you feel about who they are. Ask them to be your mentor. Take the step, even if it is the president of a corporation.

Remember, nothing ventured, nothing gained. In this world full of people from all backgrounds and walks of life, you are bound to find someone that you admire that can be reached. Don't stop until you find someone who will give you some time. It will make a difference.

27. LAUGH

Invest in a good comical movie or go to a clean comedy show. Buy or rent CD's from past eras, people like "Bob Hope," "Red Skelton," "Moms Mabley," "Flip Wilson," "Carol Burnett," "Dom DeLuise," "Jackie Gleason," "Vickie Lawrence," "Betty White," etc., you get the picture. You need to do a series of laughter marathons. Take a week and explore a different comedian each night and you will find that laughter is good for you, and it was a much-needed diversion.

28. TAKE YOURSELF OUT TO LUNCH OR DINNER

101 Ways to Keep Going, When the Going Gets Tough!

This time don't take yourself to a familiar place. Find a restaurant that you have never visited before, even better, one that you haven't even thought about patronizing at all. Take in the atmosphere. What's on the walls? Evaluate the friendliness of the waiters/waitresses. Be polite. Ask questions. Try a sample of something new (usually, you can get to taste something on the menu before you order it, but you must ask). Open your journal while you are here and write down any thoughts that come to mind.

29. COUNT YOUR BLESSINGS

Even though you may not think there is anything to be thankful for, sit down, and give yourself some time to reflect on everything about your life that is going well. Not everything is a bust. As the things that are right with your life start to penetrate your thoughts, start thanking God for those things. Thank Him again and again and then thank Him for your life and your pain. Yes, your pain, because you are learning from your pain and whether you realize it now or not, it is helping you to grow up.

30. CHANGE WHAT YOU SEE

Look for a picture that causes calmness inside of you and gives you hope, one that lifts your spirit. Enlarge that picture and put it where you can see it when you first wake up in the morning. Put it in your bathroom and even on your refrigerator. You need to keep something positive in your eyesight.

31. USE YOUR MENTAL ABILITIES TO THINK ON THE FOLLOWING THINGS:

Whatsoever things that are honest, true, just, pure, lovely, are of good report; if there is any virtue or praiseworthiness, think on these things. Should anything else try to crowd your thoughts or enter into your thoughts, cast them out. It's time to use your "thinking" capacity for greater things. Who do you know that demonstrates honesty in his/her character? Who personifies kindness? Who shows great compassion? Who's a good listener, a good friend? As you reflect on these persons, ask yourself, do any of these people's personalities have a common thread. If you can hone in on it, what is that common element?

32. DO A SELF ASSESSMENT OF YOUR ABILITIES AND SKILLS.

Make a list of everything you know how to do. Then reorganize the list with what you are best at and put it on the top. Do a little research and find out just how much that skill is worth when packaged correctly.

33. GIVE YOUR SELF A PEP TALK

Yes, there are times that you must encourage yourself. Don't be ashamed to tell yourself to stand up, sit up, shut up, whatever you need in order to bring into focus what you need to hear in order to pep up and get up from the depths of despair.

34. IT'S NO USE; I'M NO GOOD, I GIVE UP

Remove these words from your vocabulary. Ask God to forgive you for thinking this way about yourself. You are somebody because a perfect God made you. Yes, it was man who messed up, and he did have help from the devil. But even so, a perfect way has been made to restore you to your former good. Repent from useless thoughts concerning yourself and your life. You were designed for greater things, and now is the time to start believing in this truth.

CHAPTER 1 NOTES:

Dr. Marci Tilghman-Bryant

CHAPTER 2

Become Even More Determined, Boot Camp

Life has taught me some interesting things about problems. Learning these lessons has helped me keep going. Perhaps it will do the same for you.

First, problems have endurance. You can run, but they won't run with you. They just stay put, right there, and wait for you to tire yourself out. Problems love it when you are tired because you are less likely to fight back. It's like being on the ropes in a boxing ring. The tired boxer tries his best to cover up and block the blows, but he also knows if he has any chance of winning, he can't stay on the ropes. He's got to get out of the way of those punches. You can run from your problems, but you must get out of their way so you can look at them and face them head-on.

Secondly, problems have X-ray vision. You can hide behind others, or bury your head in the sand, but they will still find you. It doesn't matter where you go, or even if you change jobs, or churches, or even neighborhoods, problems just seem to tag along. So, hiding is definitely not the answer.

Third, they have tenacity. You can ignore them, but sooner or later, they will be heard loud and clear, they will not be ignored. The longer you ignore them the louder and harsher they become until not only you know they are there, but other people around you will begin to pick up on them as well.

Fourth, they have radar. You can pass them off on someone else, but they will find their way back to you. Have you ever tried to involve someone else in fixing your problem? How did that work out for you? Other people's solutions are often like band-aids, it's a temporary fix. Temporary is not what you want.

Fifth, they are selfish…yes, problems are

selfish. They want all your time. The more you talk about them, the more they love it. It keeps them hanging onto your life while others are slowly moving away.

Sixth, problems are companion oriented. They just love cohabitating with you. They love keeping you up at night, pacing the floor, or tossing and turning all night long in bed. They love breaking your concentration in the middle of the day while you are trying to attend to important matters at work or with family.

Problems hope that you never come to the **Seventh** awareness about them. They want you in the dark. But if you can find your way to number 7, the number of completion, you can turn any situation around. What is number 7? I am glad you asked!!!

Your **problems are COWARDS**. You can face them head-on!!! Tell them what they don't know…tell them who you are. You are a

M.O.U.S.E. Major **O**pposition **U**sing **S**piritual **E**quipment (the word of God)!

Tell them what they should know but obviously don't know…tell them who they are **really** messing with! You do not belong to yourself. **You belong to God**. He states in His word that if you make your bed in Hell, He is right there. He also said that He will never leave you or forsake you and that He would be with you until the end of this world. He has assigned angels all around you. You are not alone and your weapons of warfare are not carnal. He said for you to call and He will answer. Use the power in God's word. Say His words out loud. Use your faith by standing firm in what He has said in His word to you. Believe in the victory from God's word even though you can't readily see it in the situation.

Tell your problem(s) what they need to know… **Back up, back off, back out, & back down!** Your problems have occupied your territory one minute too long. It's time they were put on the run.

Then really throw them a curveball. Tell those problems who they really are…**NOTHING** but a light thing. Because they were no match for Jesus in the past, or in the present and will never be in the future, claim your victory now!

Yes, you are victorious over these problems. Romans 8:37 says that we are more than conquers through Him who loved us. Don't let problems steal any more of your precious time. Face them.

35. SET A GOAL THAT IS ATTAINABLE.

We all need something to challenge us once in a while. We were not created to be mediocre or just status quo. Perhaps you did not know that, but now you do. Pick up a new challenge today and be determined to complete the task.

36. ASSESS YOUR BELIEF SYSTEM

What is your attitude toward people, money, church, education, materialism, idealism, and realism? You need to know what you believe and why you believe. What's working for you and what is not working for you? Now is a good time to make some changes your belief system.

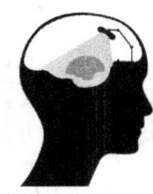

37. THINK PROGRESSION

You must move forward. Don't stay in this place. There is more to life than this moment you are in now. Live this moment to the fullest, but you must prepare for the next one and the next one and the next one. It is time to plan your next step and then go for it.

38. SELECT A PERSON WHO NEEDS CHEERING UP AND SPEND A DAY WITH THEM MAKING THEM FEEL IMPORTANT.

Yes, others need to feel like they matter, and it is your job to help them feel that way. Why is it your job? Because you too need cheering up and you need to plant cheer in order to receive cheer, so get to planting.

39. SPEAK BLESSINGS OVER THE LIFE OF SOMEONE YOU KNOW PERSONALLY WHO NEEDS A MIRACLE.

It helps you find peace within yourself when you seek to bless others. You can do this blessing by speaking out loud to the person and/or the person's circumstances. Bless them kindly with words of encouragement and comfort and pray that God will sustain them until their change comes.

40. SELECT A NEW HOBBY. YOU CAN CHOOSE, BOWLING, SEWING, JUDO, LINE DANCING, DANCE ROLLER SKATING, A FOREIGN LANGUAGE OR INTERPRETIVE, ETC.

You choose something that you know very little about but have at least once in your life have wanted to try it out. Find a mentor or tutor.

41. BREAK YOUR ROUTINE

Yes, this is hard because you are comfortable in several areas of your existence. Change your route to work, if you like a certain brand of coffee, try another. Change the place where you usually sit in order to drink your coffee to another place altogether. Experiment…Try drinking tea instead. If you are a tea drinker, change to coffee or hot chocolate. Now you get the picture. THE TASTE? Aaaarrrrgggguuuuh. I know, I know, I know, it's not gooooooood. It's not what you are accustomed to, and that's the point; it is **time for a change.**

Been going to bed at 10 pm, now try 9 pm or 11 pm. Been getting up at 7 am…Now try 6 or 6:30 am. Where do you shop for groceries? Try to go to a different supermarket.

What's your favorite department store? Try one that you have never entered before.

42. SURF THE INTERNET

This superhighway/internet has a vast amount of information about practically anything you can imagine. However, this exercise is meant to help you heal and look forward to your future with hope and great expectations, so use the search engines to look for information about positive things that interest you. One good suggestion is to type in "inspirational quotes." Another suggestion would be "greatest American poets & poetry," you can also type in what you are feeling or longing for, i.e., "how to deal with aloneness," "ways to overcome disappointments," etc.

43. GO TO A RARE BOOKSTORE OR A RESALE SHOP

Spend a few hours looking through the different items, take the time to really look at how time has changed the everyday use of certain items that were once so popular. Spend time in a quiet atmosphere, reading and thinking. Take mental notes on whatever you find that interests you.

44. WRITE A SONG

I know you are not a songwriter. But your life is like a song, let your mind flow and go and write down what it's speaking to your heart. You might be pleasantly surprised. Give it to someone you know who sings and ask them to put a tune to those words.

45. THINK OF SOMEONE YOU NEED TO MAKE AMENDS WITH WHO IS LIVING OR DECEASED.

Write them a letter and pour out the contents of your heart. Be sincere. If the person is still alive, make every effort to get it to them. If not, God has just recorded your confession in the lambs' book of life. You will be rewarded from Him.

46. DOWNLOAD TO YOUR PHONE OR TABLET SOUNDS OF "NATURE"

Play the sounds of nature while driving your car, while relaxing at home and when you retire to bed. These sounds will come through like they never have before. These sounds will help you tune into your own awareness of what's all around you.

47. NOTHING COMES TO STAY…EVERYTHING COMES TO PASS.

Regardless of what you are feeling right now, this moment will pass and eventually, what you are feeling will pass. Remember the best joke you ever heard? Remember how hard and hardy you laughed and laughed? It seemed as if the laughter would never end, but it did, didn't it? This pain or disappointment or sadness you feel right now works in the same cycle that did that great laughing experience: It will pass. Believe that NOW.

48. ALL YOU SEE NOW IS THE CLOSED DOOR...OPEN YOUR EYES WIDE.

Whenever a door closes, another one always opens up. We often spend too much time looking at the closed door that we miss, the open one which will lead to new experiences and adventures. There is a new path, look for it, and then follow it.

49. PAIN, SORROW, GRIEF, DISAPPOINTMENT, ANGER, AND HUMILIATION

Is all a part of this earthly life. These feelings of woe often bring us to the brink of despair and the feeling of hopelessness. But there is light at the end of each chapter. When you feel like it's useless to keep going, bring into your consciousness the reason WHY you have held on so long until now. That reason is your lifeline, for now, so keep going.

50. WHAT IS THE END OF THE ROAD FOR A CATERPILLAR, THAT IS CALLED A BUTTERFLY WITH WINGS?

The situations and circumstances that have brought you to this place are now dead. It is often why the pain is so great. The reality is the time for change has come into your life. You can't stay here forever, and you cannot go backward, so gather the courage you need, and the strength you need, to go forward, one step at a time, one day at a time. Read the 23rd Psalm. You are a budding butterfly, and you have wings…

51. REST IF YOU MUST, BUT DON'T YOU QUIT.

"REST, IF YOU MUST, BUT DON'T YOU QUIT."

There is an anonymous poem that has been in circulation. There is an anonymous poem that has been in circulation for years. It bears repeating:

When things go Wrong as they sometimes Will,
When the Road you're Trudging seems all Up Hill,
When the Funds are Low and the Debts are High
And you want to Smile, but you have to Sigh,
When Care is Pressing you Down a Bit,
REST! IF YOU MUST;
BUT DON'T YOU QUIT!

Life is Queer with its Twists and Turns,
As every one of us Sometimes Learns,
And many a Failure Turns About
When he might have Won had he Stuck it Out;
DON'T GIVE UP though the Pace seems Slow;
But you may Succeed with another Blow.
Often the is Near Than
It seems to a Faint and Faltering Man

Often the Struggler has GIVEN UP
When he might have Captured the Victor's Cup

And he Learned TOO LATE when the
Night Slipped Down
How close he was to the GOLDEN CROWN

Success is FAILURE Turned Inside Out;
The Silver Tint of the Clouds of Doubt,
And you NEVER can tell How Close you are,
It may be Near when it seems Afar;

So, STICK to the Fight
When you're Hardest Hit;
It's when things seem Worst
THAT YOU MUST NOT QUIT.

52. SO, YOU HAVE FALLEN AGAIN; THIS MAKES THE 7TH TIME.

You got up before; get up again for the 8th time around! But this time hold on to the lessons you have learned and be determined not to repeat the mistakes.

53. REMEMBER BACK WHEN YOU USED TO DREAM ABOUT WHAT YOU WERE GOING TO DO SOMEDAY?

It is now someday. Pick up at least one piece of that dream and begin to dream again. Add to the dream continually until the whole picture comes into view; then you proceed to live your dream. Remember, we all need a vision to keep going.

54. IF WHERE YOU ARE RIGHT NOW FEELS LIKE HELL, KEEP MOVING.

To be successful in this life there is no layover or stopover in Hell. Get out & get out fast! How? Don't sit there and wallow day in and day out, get to stepping toward your future. God created you with a plan in mind and you won't find it sitting still wallowing in self-pity. Go to church.

55. STOP TRYING TO FIND SOMEONE TO BLAME.

If you have come to this place, you have played your part and it is because of your own actions. Yes, others may have played a part but so did you, whether you are willing to admit it or not. Now, what have you learned from this experience? If by some small chance that you are at this place solely because of the actions of another, then take a good hard look at what you have learned from this experience? People make mistakes and people sometimes hurt other people. Sometimes it is intentional, sometimes it's not. But the point is, blaming someone, anyone at this point is of little value, and it will do nothing to jumpstart your life. Forgive yourself and forgive others.

56. YOU ARE THE SUM TOTAL OF WHAT YOU BELIEVE.

But what you believe may not be what you were created to become. God created all living creatures and man what gifted with the highest honor of all, greatness and a "WILL" of His own. You were destined to come into your own purpose, but along the way, you have run into some stags, roadblocks, and bends in the road. While these may slow you down, they don't have to keep you from your destiny. Change your thoughts about yourself today. You are somebody. You are who God made you to be even though you may not have arrived. The journey is not yet over.

57. NO ONE GETS LOST ON A STRAIGHT PATH.

Decide for yourself a course. You are here. Where do you want to get to, and how long do you want to take to get there? Write it down. Draw a line from where you are to where you want to go. Let nothing sidetrack you. Take your first step and keep the goal in front of you. Take the next step, then the next step, then the next step. You will be amazed at just how short the journey really is overall.

58. LET ANGER GO

It only ends in cruelty. You can live without it. No one can do it for you; you must make the conscious choice not to let anger remain in control of your life. Anger leads to greater offensives that can mar your life. Read Psalms 87, verses 8 and 9.

59. DON'T KEEP LETTING YESTERDAY'S TRIALS AND HURT USE UP TOO MUCH OF YOUR TODAY.

Yesterday is gone, and it will never come back again. It only exists in your memory. Keep the lessons learned, the happy memories, and let the rest go. You have tomorrow to aim for and you must start towards it today.

60. THE BIRD WHO HAS EATEN HIMSELF TO GLUTTONY CANNOT FLY WITH THE BIRD WHO IS HUNGRY

Are you full and lazy with cares of the past, or are you in great need to get filled with love, peace, and joy that sits just beyond the horizon? If you want it go for it, there aren't any weights holding you down, unless…you stop trying or you stop believing.

61. LISTEN

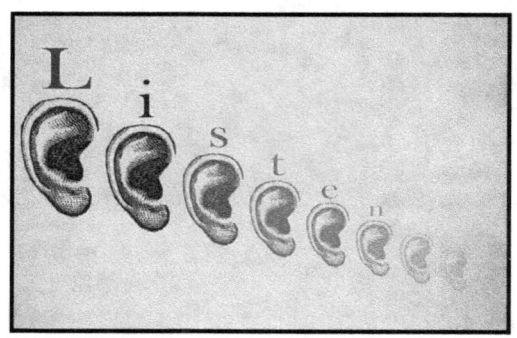

Sometimes we can just talk too much and not hear what is being said. It's important to hear what thus saith the Lord. Besides, if you don't ever stop to listen, your own tongue will make you deaf.

62. JUST AS A GEM CAN'T BE POLISHED WITHOUT FRICTION, A MAN CANNOT BE PERFECTED WITHOUT TRIALS

In this life, you shall have trials; you shall have tribulation. You can't stop it, but you can decide how you are going to deal with it. In the midst of a trial? Thank God you are growing. Now kneel down and ask him for his help to get through it.

63. WORDS HAVE NO WINGS BUT THEY CAN FLY A THOUSAND MILES OR MORE TO HIT THE INTENDED TARGET.

Watch what you say and to whom you say it. If you have wronged someone with your words, apologize. If someone has hurt you with their words, don't retaliate by hurting someone else with your words. Words are powerful. They have a life of their own once you set them free. Choose them wisely before they leave your mouth; they could be very hard to swallow if you have to take them back. Also, they sometimes can cause damage that could take a lifetime to undo.

CHAPTER 2 NOTES:

101 Ways to Keep Going, When the Going Gets Tough!

CHAPTER 3

You are Special, Boot Camp

One day, not very long ago, I received an email entitled: YOU ARE SPECIAL. I wasn't feeling very special, so my gut reaction was just to delete it and move on. But...move on to what? What better could be waiting for me than that particular message? What a great way to start a day, knowing, believing, that you are special. I am so glad that I didn't listen to my gut that day. After all, my gut was in the cellar and my gut wanted me to stay there. Thank God there was that small still voice telling me to listen, listen, listen.

You have a small still voice inside of you too. Stop trying to silence it. It's only trying the help you. Those words I chose to read that day helped me to move another step forward, so now I share them with you.

I. ***Even though I clutch my blanket and growl*** when the alarm rings; thank You, Lord, that I can hear; there are many who are deaf.

II. ***Even though I keep my eyes closed*** against the morning light as long as possible, thank you Lord again; that I can see; for many are blind.

III. ***Even though, at times the first hour of my day*** is hectic, when socks are lost, toast is burned and tempers are short, and the children are so loud; thank you Lord for my family; there are many who are estranged from their family, alone and lonely.

IV. ***Even though the breakfast table never looks*** like the pictures in magazines and the menus are often unbalanced, thank you Lord, for the food we have; for there are many who go to bed hungry and awaken to that same condition…

V. ***Even though the routine of my job*** is often monotonous, thank you, Lord, for the opportunity to work, to earn a living, for there are many who have no job.

VI. ***Even though I report to a boss*** who sometimes (maybe oftentimes) seem cruel, unreasonable, impractical, and insensitive, thank you Lord, for I know my worth and my future lies not in my boss's hands, but yours!

VII. ***Even though I sometimes grumble*** and bemoan my fate from day to day and wish my circumstances were not so difficult or modest, thank you, Lord, for life, for many have already departed this state of consciousness and have gone on to the afterlife.

VIII. ***Even though I don't always feel like smiling*** because of disappointments or pain thank you, Lord, for it costs me nothing to do it, and it just may brighten someone else's day, for many others may be hurting too.

IX. ***If we can pass on a word or a message of hope to just one person every day,*** someone we know or don't know except a chance meeting, it just might help to make this world a better place to live right now.

X. ***Many of us are still on this journey.*** Don't travel through aimlessly. Travel with purpose. So, thank the Lord for the opportunity to make someone else's day and perhaps you will make someone else's burden just a little nicer and a little lighter. Thank you, Lord, for reminding me that I AM SPECIAL

The essences of these well wishes were adjusted a little by me in order to grab and hold your attention. It's important that you know I understand where you are and what you might be going through, at least where your feelings are concerned. We all feel, and we all need comforting.

Pain, sorrow, disappointments transcend our social and financial status. These emotions find every soul, rich, poor, educated, uneducated, and certainly, race plays no factor. One of the many gifts that we are endowed with is the gift of friendship. Be a friend to yourself first, then find someone who needs a friend and become one.

64. A MAN'S AFFAIRS ARE EVALUATED AFTER HIS COFFIN IS CLOSED.

You are not dead yet. Your coffin is still empty. Life belongs to you. Live, my friend, live! You still have not completed all your affairs. There is more to do and more to put in order. Look within to find your destiny. Rest if you must, but just make up your mind that you won't quit. A young man I used to know once said to a group of us long before he died, "in this life, you will either wear out or rust out; I choose to wear out!" He kept on living and doing all the days of his life.

65. GO BIKE RIDING OR JOGGING

You can do this alone or with some friends. But do it. The exercise will be good for you and the wind in your face just might make you remember what it was like when you were a kid, riding your bike like you didn't have a care in the world.

66. BREAK THE BONDAGE THAT HOLDS YOU.

Read Romans Chapter 12 in the New Testament of the Bible. Remember, specifically that there is now no condemnation to them (you)…You do not live under the law, but under grace. Don't continue to repeat your mistakes and don't continue to feel guilty over them either. Once you have been forgiven by God, nothing else really matters. He holds your future, not anyone else.

67. PURCHASE A BOX OF "THINKING OF YOU" CARDS.

Sit down and address one to everyone you can think of that you owe a debt of gratitude for the something they did for you, not just the grand gestures but the small ones too. They all have helped to bring you to this place.

68. PICK ONE ROOM OR ONE SMALL SPACE WHERE YOU LIVE AND REDECORATE IT.

The goal here is to create an atmosphere of peace & tranquility. What will make this space peaceful? What will make it feel warm and inviting? Do it! God gave you a wonderful imagination now is the time to use it; you know what fragrances you like; you know what calms you. Just remember, this is the space where you will meet with God.

69. VISIT AN ARTS AND CRAFTS STORE.
Purchase a watercolor tablet that gives you pictures that you can paint by color. Elementary, but it will work in order to help you create some beautiful pictures. You need to surround yourself with some things that you have created. Don't forget to purchase the paints and brushes as well.

70. YOU ARE NOT A VICTIM
Stop acting like one. You are more than a conqueror. Whatever has happened, while the pain of it lingers now, you are a better, stronger person for having survived this episode in your life.

Somebody, somewhere else in this world is worse off than you. Be grateful that you are still in control of your destiny.

71. YOU ARE NOT A FAILURE

Just because some aspect of your life has not blossomed as you had hoped doesn't make YOU the failure. The mission failed. You now have the unique opportunity to examine yourself and all the efforts and elements that caused this to come out the way it has. If the venture was worth having, then perhaps the method by which you chose to get there was wrong. Try again and this time do your homework. Pray and proceed with caution.

72. WALK INTO GOD'S HOLY PRESENCE.

But do so with something to sacrifice. Give Him praise from your lips for who He is. Give Him your undivided attention. Turn off the TV, the cell phone, or the radio. Worship Him with your whole heart. Forget about yourself for this period of time and just concentrate on Him. Go to that special place that you have created just for you and Him. (#67)

73. WHO IS YOUR MASTER?

Whatever or whoever is controlling your actions, thoughts, and desires is your master. You need to know who or what is most important to you. Material things cannot be your God if you expect an eternal return. Other people cannot be your God unless you are willing to settle for a lifetime of disappointment. You certainly don't want the devil or demons to be in control of your life; that would be pure torment. So, there is only one real choice, will you make Jesus your choice today?

74. THIS IS YOUR PERSONAL JOURNEY

Everyone you meet along life's highway will not be on this journey with you. Some will walk with you or ride with you for a while but make no mistake, once their purpose in your life is fulfilled, they will move on. So, should you.

75. STOP MAKING EXCUSES FOR YOURSELF AND OTHERS.

Excuses never did one thing to change or fix any situation; action does. Take action. Own your part, make your amends, and let it go so that you can move forward. Don't take anyone else's burden on your shoulders.

76. STOP LISTENING TO THE ENEMY

Anyone who is not for you is against you. Anyone who is not rowing in the same direction as you are has a different purpose. Don't be offended because they can no longer walk with you…Besides, the real truth is that you can no longer walk with them; you are not speaking the same language. So, whatever their conversation, you have outgrown it and your path is in another direction. Stop letting them tell you where you should go and go where your path leads.

77. CONNECT

You must be able to be connected to yourself before you can harmoniously connect to others? Who are you? Do you know? Take out a sheet of paper and go to your quiet place. Divide the paper into two parts. On the left side of the paper, write down those things about yourself that you like. On the right side of the paper, write down those things that you know about yourself that you do not like. Then on the reverse side of the paper, write down those things that others have told you about yourself, good or bad. Then compare that list to the list on the front. As you begin to do this exercise, it will force you to take a look at who you are versus who you think you are. Are there any aspects of what you have just discovered that you want to change? If so, just know that you can.

78. YOUR CHOICES DEFINE YOU

Take a good long look at the recent choices that you have made. Are you working at a job that you like? Are you living in the neighborhood or in the type of dwelling you desire? Are you driving the car of your choice? Do you even own a car? Do you have a driver's license? What have you accomplished since you left high school? What types of food do you like? What types of entertainment hold your interest? Answer these questions. Now that you are looking circumspectly at the choices you have made, are you ready now to make some different ones?

79. TAKE A TRIP TO A NEIGHBORING STATE

Take a day, get in your car and ride. If you do not drive, buy a bus ticket or train ticket and go to the next state. Prior to leaving town, make a hotel reservation at a hotel of your choice for at least a two-night stay. Preferably, pick a hotel that offers room service. Pamper yourself at least for one day and one night; break away from the norm. Find out what the local attraction is to the hotel you are staying in and go there. Treat yourself to a date with yourself.

80. WRITE DOWN THE CURRENT VISION OF YOUR LIFE.

What is lifelike for you right now, in this moment? Pain, disappointment, sadness, emptiness, all this, like everything else in life comes to…pass; not to stay. Your challenge is to get past today by living today and every day after today, one day at a time. Now write down one thing that you would like to change and meditate on it.

81. FIND YOUR PASSION

Everyone needs a reason to be alive, something

that charges them up and puts them into action. Align yourself with others who are passionate about the same things that you are passionate about. Making new friends is easier when you have something in common. Go to places that interest you. Read books that interest you. Listen to music that stirs your soul. Find your groove and settle into it. You will be amazed at how far you go and how much better you will feel.

82. CHANGE YOUR FOCUS

You are not a loser. Losers tend to focus on what they are going through. Take a deep breath and focus on where you are going to from here. Remind yourself of that aspect of your life that you want to change (#80). What is your first step? Take it, after all, the journey of a thousand miles begins with the first step.

CHAPTER 3 NOTES:

Dr. Marci Tilghman-Bryant

CHAPTER 4

Common Ground, Boot Camp

I recently read a large poster that was situated in a very public place and it moved me. When I made reference to it to some other colleagues who worked in that environment every day, they told me that they never noticed it before. I couldn't imagine being in that place every day and not noticing it, yet I came to realize that we as humans, often overlook precious things. We are not always aware of our surroundings.

The sign read:

He Prayed – I didn't, It was not my religion.

He Spoke – I didn't Answer, It was not my Language.

He Was Dressed – So was I, But our clothes were very different.

He Ate – I did not, His food was different than what I was accustomed too.

He Smiled – I Smiled

He Laughed – I Laughed

He Cried – I Cried

Without words…we found common ground. We communicated.

Sometimes words are not what we need in order to communicate. We just need to know someone cares. And someone does care about you! But you must care about yourself as well. Feeling sorry for yourself will never get you to the place of fulfillment where you want and need to be. Perhaps it is time to forgive yourself. You can't change your past, but you can do something about your future. And you must start where you are, in your present!

83. TAKE A LEGAL ASSESSMENT OF WHAT IS YOURS, THEN TAKE A SPIRITUAL ASSESSMENT OF WHAT IS YOURS.

In the material world you are the total of your assets. What do you own? What do you owe? The difference is your net worth. As for the spiritual assessment, you will need to search the scriptures. Start with the book of Genesis in the Holy Bible, Chapters 1 and 2. Then read the book John (4th book in the New Testament) Chapter 1. Read the book of Romans, Chapter 8 and Romans, Chapter 12. Read Ephesians Chapter 6. These readings are only the beginning. Take some Bible reading time daily. Try to commit to at least 30 minutes a day.

84. YOUR MIND IS A BATTLEFIELD

The thoughts that come to your mind are either healthy which lead to healing, or they are morbid which leads to sickness. Many of the physical illnesses we experience are a result of stress, pain, heartache, and overwhelming sadness. You need to understand that your mind is impartial. It is non-judgmental. It has an amazing ability to conform.

It will accept what you put into it. It feeds on what you give it. It fuels your imagination. Your thoughts will shape your future. As difficult as it is, you must stop allowing your mind to rest on morbid and painful thoughts.

85. LOOK FOR THE PRIZE

Every dark day, every dark cloud has a silver lining. Things really are not as bad as they seem. There is always a light at the end of the tunnel. Where you are at the moment may be too deep to see the prize (which is also the light). Make up in your mind and in your heart to keep going for the prize. Keep on living.

86. YOU CAN NOT LIVE IN THE PAST.

Yesterday is gone. Everything but the memory of it has left your life! You can never go back. You cannot undo anything that was done or said. But you have the gift of the present. It is today and today is another opportunity to mend. Life is very precious; your life is precious. You have the right to be here because God has willed it to be so. There is a purpose in the earth for you. Find your purpose. It is ahead of you, not behind you. PRAY.

87. YOUR MESS IS A MESSAGE.

Right now, you are learning a valuable lesson. The lesson is meant to be shared because it will help somebody else in your future. Take a good long look at everything that has brought you to this place. What part did you contribute? What could you or should you have done differently? You will be tested again, so be sure that you are committed to not repeating the same mistake(s). Then as you move on, you will get the opportunity to show someone else or tell someone else how not to go down the path you just encountered. In other words, you will be a blessing to someone else.

88. STOP MOANING AND COMPLAINING

This battle may not have been one of your choosing, but the outcome of this battle is your choice. You can win it by staying on the Lord's side, reading and following His word, and giving Him praise, or you can wallow in self-pity. Wallowing in self-pity is a sure way of keeping the battle in the hands of your enemy. It's time to take back the controls of your life that you handed over to someone else.

89. GIVE YOURSELF A BREAK.

Give everything that concerns you over to God. It's time to stop wrestling and start resting. Face it. There are just some things in this life you do not have any control over. Until you have a certain knowledge base, certain decisions were not made clear. Until you had a deeper understanding about life and your particular circumstances, you may not have been able to foresee certain consequences. But now you do. Thank God that you have come to this point of understanding. Ask Him to help you get beyond it.

90. TAKE INVENTORY OF YOUR SPIRITUAL LIFE.

Do not evaluate your spiritual maturity/growth in terms of money. Luke 12:15 tells us that a man's life does not consist in the abundance of the things he possesses materially. Rich, poor, or somewhere in between does not establish who you are or where you are with your relationship to God through his Son, Jesus Christ. Do not evaluate your spirituality based on your popularity or your fame. All of us are humans and we all go out of this world eventually, by the same path. Our wealth nor our fame will prevent our earthly departure, for it is written in the Bible that it is appointed unto man once to die, and after this the resurrection unto eternal life, or you can spend your eternity totally separated from God.

And lastly, do not evaluate your life based on the grief, pain, or sufferings you have experienced. Tears are certain in this life, starting with our birth. Things happen, disappointments come. We are deeply affected by what happens in our experience.

> Trouble comes, but trouble doesn't last always. In Psalm 30 Verse 5, it reads in part…" weeping may endure for a night, but joy comes in the morning."

Hold on to this truth. There is still joy on the horizon just look for it.

91. GET READY TO GO WITH GOD TO A BRAND-NEW PLACE.

Set your sight on the presence and power of God. Follow where He is leading you; stop trying to get there all by yourself. God made you and He knows where He wants you to go; just follow, after all, He does know the way. Trust Him.

92. SANCTIFY YOURSELF

Clean up your act! Get rid of the sin in your life that has separated you from God. Even though everything inside of you is crying out that you can't, you can by letting go of all your own efforts and trusting in Jesus. He is your righteousness, and He has paid the price for your sins. He is your strength and your way back to the Father. Wake up! You have tried everything else; now it's time to put your faith and dependence on the one true "Way" …God's way. Make up your mind not to go back to where you have just come from. Believe that there is another way more excellent than any you have tried and follow that new way. You may get your feet wet, but there is dry land ahead.

93. GOD IS ON YOUR SIDE.

If God be for you, He is more than the world against you. When God is on your side, it does not matter who or what is against you! If God were not on your side, it wouldn't matter who or what is. Go with God. He is the sure win!

94. P.R.A.Y.E.R.

Petition **R**ighteously to **A**lmighty God for **Y**our every need **E**very day **R**everently! Don't forget to thank God for all the goodness and blessings that He has bestowed upon your life. Thanksgiving is just as important as asking for your daily needs.

95. LET'S GO BIBLE SHOPPING

Let's go on an adventure together. Dig into the scriptures to find those verses that speak to your heart and give you hope and strength. Let's write them down (chapter and verse) and commit them to memory so that we can say them as often as we need to in order to keep going and growing in God's grace.

96. STAND OUT

It may surprise you to learn that God expects those who belong to Him to **Stand Out**, <u>not</u> just *fit in*. In the Bible, Christians are described as the "Lights in this World" and the "Salt of the Earth." Read Matthew Chapter 5. We are also described as a peculiar people (1 Peter 2:9). We indeed are not like everybody else, so we should stop trying to blend in.

97. TODAY IS THE FIRST DAY OF THE REST OF YOUR LIFE.

You have a choice in how your life unfolds. You can make changes and you have the help and support you need to do so.

98. DON'T THROW IN THE TOWEL.

You are not all washed up. Don't give up, don't give in, don't give out. The only one who wins if you do this is the enemy of your soul. You came here for a purpose and it shall be done in your life if you don't give up.

99. FORGIVE AND FORGET THE OFFENSE BUT NOT THE LESSON

Yes, offenses come. People have hurt you. But you have also hurt others, perhaps not deliberately, but it has happened. God forgives us, so we have no choice but to forgive if we want to be set free from bondage. Forgiveness is a must if we are to be successful in moving our life forward. Some people say it's hard to forgive but think about it. Take the sins of the whole world and think about the supreme sacrifice that Jesus made to ensure that you and I would have the right to reclaim our eternal heritage. It took a lot of forgiveness and love and to die in "everyone's" place. If God forgave us "all" and put our sins against Him in a sea of forgetfulness, surely, we can forgive and forget the offenses of the few people that we have come to know in this lifetime.

100. LISTEN FOR YOUR DRUMMER.

Do you hear the distant drummer? He is tapping out the rhythm for your life. I have heard the distant drummer all my life, but until I matured in certain areas of my life, I could not clearly discern the drumbeat. There was a path that was mine to follow. There is a path that you are to follow. I am not to follow yours; you are not to follow mine; we, are not to follow anybody else's. But we will get where we are going together. We need to be on the Lord's side at all times and His leading will get us to every promise and every gift that has been given to us.

101. THE SIGNATURE…JESUS IS…

Our Lord, our peace, our forgiveness, our love, our fellowship, our example, our security, our strength, our sufficiency, our fulfillment, our righteousness, our contentment, our friend, and our everything. He will be what you need Him to be. But you must let Him in.

I sincerely hope that you have enjoyed this journey with me. It has been my joy to share with you these wonderful revelations that have helped me keep on moving. Finally, but not at all the end of things, let me remind you that…

Payday is on the way. It's time to take your life

back! So, take FIVE, the number of "grace." Grace is amazing, Grace is sufficient, Grace is favor, Grace is good, Grace belongs to you as a part of your eternal heritage!

CHAPTER 4 NOTES:

101 Ways to Keep Going, When the Going Gets Tough!

WHO IS JESUS?

The Word of God
Became Flesh…

The Son of God
Became a Man…

The Lord of All
Became a Servant…

The Righteous One
Became Sin…

The Eternal One
Came and tasted Death…

The Risen One
Came from Heaven and went back to Heaven…

The Chosen One

Came to live in Man and guide Him…

The Seated One

Is Coming Back Again For His Bride…the church!

WILL YOU BE READY???

Dr. Marci Tilghman-Bryant

CONTACT INFORMATION

CONTACT OUR MINISTRY
@ 888-996-0696

BVT Ministries Outreach
Bellevue CC 510 Duncan Road, #306,
Wilmington, DE 19809

If our ministry can be of service to your ministry, please contact us. Elder Bryant is available for conducting seminars, speaking engagements, and planning, including:

- LET THE OPPRESSED GO FREE
- THE 40 DAY MIND FAST SERIES
- UNDO THE HEAVY BURDENS
- DEAL THY BREAD TO THE HUNGRY
- LOOSE THE BANDS OF WICKEDNESS
- THE DYNAMIC WOMAN

- THY RIGHTEOUSNESS SHALL GO BEFORE THEE
- RIDE UPON THE HIGH PLACES

There are 50 seminars in this collection of teaching. Listed above are some of the most requested ones. You can request a complete seminar listing by going directly to our website and emailing us at **drmeb2004@yahoo.com**. Consider hosting one at your church.

We also have drama fundraisers!

Dr. Marci Tilghman-Bryant

MAY THE POEM BELOW

BLESS YOU TODAY

FROM MY HEART TO YOURS…

GOD SENT HIS SON MY WAY

My Life was in Ruin and much Decay
All my Good was just Plain Bad
There were No Joy Bells, No Merry Songs
And my Heart was So Very Sad

Not a Single Hero
Could I find Among Men
For all shared the same lot
The same Sad Place that I was in

I was Shackled with Burdens
Most of them Untold
They Weighed me Down
And caused Heaviness in my Soul

The World sent me Wolves

Wrapped up as Sheep

They Tore my Life Apart;

And Robbed me of my Sleep

The World gave me Woe

Instead of Loving Care;

Love was all I asked for

But I COULD NOT find it Anywhere

I had No Mind to Pray for myself

I was Dying Inside & Out;

For my Turmoil was Great

Nothing Left to Shout About

Then someone, somewhere

Obeyed the Master & Performed His Will;

They folded their Hands and Prayed

That I would find His Holy Hill

Someone, for me
Took the time to Pray
That God would send His Son
My Way

When Jesus came
I was Wounded and Broken
Not who I used to be
Not even a Shadow or Token

Jesus picked up the Pieces
Of my Shattered Vase
Remolded my life
And put a Smile on my Face

I must thank God Each and Everyday
For He in His Perfect Love for me…
SENT HIS SON MY WAY!

By Dr. Marci Tilghman-Bryant

ABOUT THE AUTHOR

Dr. Marci Tilghman-Bryant "Dr. Marci"
A personal mentor

Dr. Marci Tilghman-Bryant is a personal mentor. She independently organized and developed teaching seminars to benefit community and church leaders, and individuals in startup business ventures.

She left her employment as a teacher in the public-school system in 2011 to devote her efforts to training others full-time in growing their personal passions and business goals. Her team of professionals can provide the most value and innovation per dollar that you spend by providing exceptional value for each training service provided. She holds five degrees including a double Master's in Educational Leadership and Christian Ministry

Education, and a Doctorate in Ministry. She is a certified Life Coach Facilitator. She is the host of Power Up TV talk show that airs over the Phillycam Network as well as the Nazca/Roku Network and The NOW Network. She is also a published author. Her books include, "No Need to Run," "Will the Laughter Come Again," & "101 Ways to Keep Going When the Going gets Tough!" available on Amazon and directly from her websites as well. She currently serves as the Branch President in Wilmington, DE for the Freedom Bible College & Seminary.

Dr. Marci is the founder of Building the Virtuous Temple Ministries whose mission is to teach sound biblical doctrine and to train men and women in all phases o ministry. She is the director of the BVT School of Ministry; Dr. Marci Bryant Ministries is a part of its international outreach. She works with pastors, missionaries, and leaders across the nation and in other countries such as Australia, Canada, England, France, Ghana, Italy, and Nigeria.

Photo References:

- www.allanbevere.com
- www.thealternativedaily.com
- Dr. Marci Tilghman-Bryant
- www.career.iresearhnet.com
- www.christinus.wordpress
- www.chieoutsiders.com
- www.dailyprintablecalendar.com
- https://dixietanmemorial.wordpress.com/category/history/
- www.dmarge.com
- www.familypedia.wikia.com
- www.flickr.com
- www.foxnews.com
- www.huffingtonpost.com
- www.newsday.com
- www.pinterest.com
- www.pixelsquid.com
- www.pxhere.com
- www.smpsjax.com
- www.thriftyfun.com
- www.unsplash.com
- www.wallpapers13.com

www.ingramcontent.com/pod-product-compliance
Lightning Source LLC
Chambersburg PA
CBHW071501070526
44578CB00001B/406